The Exclusive Harry Potter Cookbook

30 Exquisite Recipes from Hogwarts

Delicious Meals for every Harry Potter Enthusiast

BY

Ina Deen

Table of Contents

Recipe 1 - Golden Snitch Cake

For great events and special birthday parties, this cake is the best surprise you can easily arrange at home. Inspired from original Golden snitch this cake is loaded with yellow icing. Add paper wings to the sides, and it will look as real as the Harry Potter series. To add more details, make swirling patterns on the outer layer of icing using a piping tip.

Serving Size: 10

Prep Time: 20 minutes

Total Prep Time: 32 minutes

List of Ingredients:

For Cake:

- 2/3 cup coconut flour
- ½ cup cocoa powder
- ½ tsp. baking soda
- ½ tsp. salt
- ½ cup plain Greek yogurt
- 3/4 cup honey
- 6 eggs
- ½ cup water
- 1 Tbsp. vanilla extract

For the butterscotch frosting:

- 3 egg whites
- ½ cup 2 Tbsp. coconut sugar
- 1 cup butter,
- 1 tsp. vanilla extract
- 2 Tbsp. butterscotch schnapps
- pinch of salt
- 4 drops yellow food coloring
- gold pearl dust

For the wings:

- template for tracing
- 1 large piece of scrapbook paper (silver or gold)
- 2 lollipop sticks
- hot glue

xxxxxxxxxxxxxxxxxxxxxxxxxxxxxxxxxxxxxxxxxxxxxx

Methods:

For chocolate cake:

1. Set the oven to 350 degrees F.

2. Grease two ovenproof glass bowls with oil.

3. Mix coconut flour with baking soda, salt and cocoa powder in a bowl.

4. Beat yogurt with honey in a mixer until smooth. Gradually add eggs while beating.

5. Stir in vanilla and water and mix well until smooth.

6. Slowly stir in flour mixture and mix until combined.

7. Divide the batter into two bowls and bake for 32 minutes.

8. Let the cakes to cool and remove from the glass bowls.

9. Wrap them in foil sheets and refrigerate for 2 hours.

For the butterscotch frosting:

10. Meanwhile, boil 2 inches of water in a saucepan.

11. Whisk egg whites with sugar in a glass bowl and place it on the simmering water.

12. Mix well until sugar is dissolved.

13. Beat the mixture until foamy.

14. Add butter then blend on low speed until mixed.

15. Stir in yellow food color and mix well to get a golden color.

For the wings:

16. Make four wings using scrapbook paper by cutting into the wing shapes.

17. Stick two wings together while putting a lollipop stick at the center to insert.

To assemble:

18. Unwrap the cakes and place one cake on the cake board with its round side down.

19. Top this cake with a dollop of frosting and place the other cake with its flat side down.

20. Coat the entire cake with one layer of frosting evenly.

21. Refrigerate the cake for 20 minutes.

22. Again, the coat the cake with the frosting and refrigerate for 20 minutes.

23. Insert wings on the sides.

24. Serve.

Recipe 2 - Butterbeer Poke Cake

This butterbeer poke cake is filled with butterscotch sauce. Baked out of stored bought cake mix, the recipe is quite simple yet unique due to the pore wise stuffing of the cake down to every inch. Due to the addition of the sauce, the cake retains its soft and moist texture.

Serving Size: 12

Prep Time: 10 minutes

Total Prep Time: 25 minutes

List of Ingredients:

- 1 vanilla cake mixes (including required ingredients)
- 1 can cream soda
- 1 cup butterscotch sauce
- ½ cup melted white chocolate
- Gold sanding sugar
- 2 cups heavy cream
- ¼ cup powdered sugar
- ¼ cup melted butter
- 1 tsp. vanilla
- 1 heath bar, chopped (or ½ cup toffee bits)

xxxxxxxxxxxxxxxxxxxxxxxxxxxxxxxxxxxxxxxxxxxx

Methods:

1. Set oven to 350 degrees F.

2. Butter a 9x13 inch baking pan.

3. Mix cake mix with cream soda and water to prepare the batter as per the instructions.

4. Bake according to the package instruction.

5. Allow the cake for cool then poke holes in the cake.

6. Pour butterscotch over the entire cake.

7. Cover and refrigerate for 2 hours.

8. Melt chocolate in a bowl and add it to the piping bag.

9. Make lightning bolts on a parchment paper and sprinkle golden sugar on top.

10. Let them cool and dry.

11. Beat heavy cream with vanilla in a mixer until foamy.

12. Stir in sugar and melted butter. Mix well.

13. Spread this mixture over the cake and top it with butterscotch, toffee bits, and lightning bolts.

14. Slice and serve.

XXXXXXXXXXXXXXXXXXXXXXXXXXXXXXXXXXXXXXXXXXXX

Recipe 3 - Butterbeer Hot Chocolate

This butterbeer hot chocolate is the late-night wintery delight which is great for Potter-themed parties. Use your creativity to decorate it more like a sparkling potion and enjoy it with the magical flavors of butterscotch. Full of calories, fats, and carbs, this drink is an energy booster for all.

Serving Size: 2

Prep Time: 10 minutes

Total Prep Time: 10 minutes

List of Ingredients:

For the Topping

- 3 Tbsp. sugar,
- 1 cup heavy cream
- ¾ tsp. imitation butter
- 1 tsp. vanilla extract
- 3 cups milk

For the Drink

- ¾ cup butterscotch chips
- 1 cup heavy cream
- 3 Tbsp. cocoa powder
- ¼ cup butterscotch sauce
- 1 tsp. butter flavor, optional
- 1 tsp. vanilla extract

XXXXXXXXXXXXXXXXXXXXXXXXXXXXXXXXXXXXXXXXXXX

Methods:

Topping:

1. Beat cream for 4 minutes until it thickens.

2. Stir in sugar, vanilla and butter then beat again until it forms peaks.

Drink:

3. Mix milk with cream in a saucepan and heat it for 2 minutes.

4. Add cocoa, butterscotch sauce, butter flavor, butterscotch chips.

5. Whisk well and boil for 10 minutes then remove it from the heat.

6. Divide the mixture into four serving mugs and top them with prepared toppings.

7. Serve.

XXXXXXXXXXXXXXXXXXXXXXXXXXXXXXXXXXXXXXXXXXXXXX

Recipe 4 - Dumbledore's Pensieve

Remember that mesmerizing Dumbledore's pensieve from the Harry Potter series? Those colorful swirls in the mystery bowl look appealing. Now you can too surprise your family with a bowl of pensieve made out of taste jelly and ice.

Serving Size: 4

Prep Time: 10 minutes

Total Prep Time: 5 minutes

List of Ingredients:

- 1 jelly packet, blue colored
- ¼ cup hot water
- 5-6 Ice cubes

xxxxxxxxxxxxxxxxxxxxxxxxxxxxxxxxxxxxxxxxxxxx

Methods:

1. Make jelly using 2/3 pack of the jelly package as per instructions on the box.

2. Allow the jelly to cool and set.

3. Mix the remaining jelly with hot water then add some ice cubes.

4. Beat well until it turns creamy.

5. Carve thin swirls in the set jelly.

6. Fill the swirls with creamy mixture.

7. Serve.

xxxxxxxxxxxxxxxxxxxxxxxxxxxxxxxxxxxxxxxxxxxx

Recipe 5 - Butterbeer Fudge

Fudge is great to serve as dessert and snack. Forget the traditional chocolate fudge and try these new butterbeer ones which are loaded with butterscotch. Add white chocolate, and the deal becomes irresistible for everyone.

Serving Size: 6

Prep Time: 10 minutes

Total Prep Time: 10 minutes

List of Ingredients:

For the Butterscotch Layer

- 2 Tbsp. butter
- 1 14-oz. can condense milk
- 3 cups butterscotch chips

For the White Chocolate Swirl

- 1/3 cup sweetened condensed milk
- ½ tsp. pure vanilla extract
- 1 cup white chocolate chips
- 1 cup marshmallow bits (optional)

xxxxxxxxxxxxxxxxxxxxxxxxxxxxxxxxxxxxxxxxxxxxxx

Methods:

1. Layer an 8-inch pan with aluminum foil and cooking spray.

2. Make the butterscotch layer:

3. Melt butter with butterscotch chips and condensed milk in a saucepan.

4. Pour this mixture into the pan and spread it evenly.

5. Make the white chocolate swirl:

6. Mix condensed milk with white chocolate chips and vanilla in a saucepan.

7. Cook until melted and mixed. Turn off the heat.

8. Pour this mixture into the pan and gently make swirls using a butter knife.

9. Refrigerate for 4 hours then slice to serve.

xxxxxxxxxxxxxxxxxxxxxxxxxxxxxxxxxxxxxxxxxxxx

Recipe 6 - Molly Weasley's Rock Cakes

These Rock cakes cookies are for Weasley's fans. This Harry Potter inspired recipe provides you the best of the best crunchy, fresh and sweet cookies. With the richness of cranberries and chocolate chips, this recipe will make you popular among all the Harry Potter fans. Try these as party snacks, after meal dessert or even for midnight cravings.

Serving Size: 18

Prep Time: 10 minutes

Total Prep Time: 12 minutes

List of Ingredients:

- ½ cup butter, cold
- 1 cup all-purpose flour
- ¼ cup sugar
- 1 tsp. baking powder
- ¼ cup dried cranberries (Craisins)
- ½ cup chocolate chips (semi-sweet)
- 1 egg, beaten
- 2 Tbsp. milk
- ¼ cup sea salted almonds, chopped roughly

xxxxxxxxxxxxxxxxxxxxxxxxxxxxxxxxxxxxxxxxxxxxx

Methods:

1. Preheat oven to 350 F

2. Sift flour with baking powder in a mixing bowl.

3. Cut in butter and mix well to get a cornmeal-like mixture.

4. Stir in cranberries, sugar, almonds and chocolate chips.

5. Beat egg with milk and pour it into the flour mixture gradually while stirring.

6. Mix well to form a firm dough.

7. Divide the dough on a cookie sheet lined with parchment paper.

8. Bake for 12 minutes.

9. Allow it cool then serve.

XXXXXXXXXXXXXXXXXXXXXXXXXXXXXXXXXXXXXXXXXXXXXXX

Recipe 7 - Butterbeer Pie

A pie is essentially important for a festive occasion and its celebration. If you are bored with traditional pie recipes, then try this butterbeer recipe which has creamy caramel filling and crispy pie crust.

Serving Size: 12

Prep Time: 10 minutes

Total Prep Time: 30 minutes

List of Ingredients:

For the Pie

- 1 (3.4-oz.) butterscotch pudding mix packet
- 1 ½ cup heavy cream
- 2 (14-oz.) refrigerated pie crusts
- ¼ cup caramel
- 1 ½ cup cold milk

For the Marshmallow Whipped Cream

- 1 cup heavy cream
- ½ cup marshmallow creme
- Gold sprinklers

xxxxxxxxxxxxxxxxxxxxxxxxxxxxxxxxxxxxxxxxxxxxxxx

Methods:

1. Set your oven to 350 degrees F. Layer a baking sheet with parchment paper.

2. Spread one pie crust and place it in a 9-inch pie plate.

3. Crimp the extra edges and prick the center with a fork.

4. Bake for 18 minutes until golden brown.

5. Spread the second pie crust and cut into a lightning bolt.

6. Place the bolt on a baking sheet and bake for 10 minutes.

7. Beat heavy cream until foamy.

8. Mix milk with pudding mix and let sit until it thickens.

9. Fold in cream and caramel. Mix well.

10. Transfer this mixture into pie crust and refrigerate for 3 hours.

11. Make Marshmallow Whipped Cream

12. Beat cream in a mixer until foamy and fold in marshmallow crème.

13. Spread this cream over the baked pie and place the lightning bolt on top.

14. Garnish golden sprinkles.

15. Serve.

XXXXXXXXXXXXXXXXXXXXXXXXXXXXXXXXXXXXXXXXXXXXXXX

Recipe 8 - Sorting Hat Pita Bread

That talking sorting hat in the Harry Potter series is one character to get excited about. Let's bring that hat into our homes while making simple pita bread. Once served this hat beautifully adorns the dinner table. Who would not like a freshly baked pita bread shaped in a life like that, I bet everyone does, especially the kids.

Serving Size: 6

Prep Time: 10 minutes

Total Prep Time: 20 minutes

List of Ingredients:

- 1 tsp. active dry yeast
- 1 tsp. sugar
- 2 ½ cups warm water
- 3 cups whole wheat flour
- 1 Tbsp. salt
- 1 Tbsp. olive oil
- 2-3 cups flour
- Making the Sorting Hat
- pita bread dough (above)
- foil
- nonstick spray

XXXXXXXXXXXXXXXXXXXXXXXXXXXXXXXXXXXXXXXXXXXX

Methods:

1. Mix sugar with warm water in a large bowl. Add yeast and let it sit for 10 minutes.

2. Add wheat flour and mix well until smooth.

3. Keep the mixture aside for 1 to 8 hours.

4. Stir in olive oil and salt. Knead the dough well for 10 minutes.

5. Cover the dough with plastic sheet and let it sit for 3 hours.

6. Meanwhile set the oven to 350 degrees F.

7. Make a large cone out of aluminum foil, about 8inch tall and 6-inch diameter at the base.

8. Grease the cone with some cooking spray on the outside.

9. Spread 2/3 of the dough into a circle and wrap it around the hat.

10. Pinch grooves for eyes, mouth, and wrinkles in the dough.

11. Place the cone on the baking sheet.

12. Bake the hat at 425 degrees F for 20 minutes until golden brown.

13. Serve.

xxxxxxxxxxxxxxxxxxxxxxxxxxxxxxxxxxxxxxxxxxxxxxx

Recipe 9 - Harry Potter Exploding Bon Bons

Bon Bon is served best as dessert. And these exploding bons bons are perfect for this particular theme. Filling with colorful icing inside and coated with vanilla icing on the outside. Decorate them with yellow lightning bolts for special effects.

Serving Size: 6

Prep Time: 10 minutes

Total Prep Time: 25 minutes

List of Ingredients:

- 1 packet vanilla cake mix, plus ingredients required
- 3/4 cups vanilla icing
- 1 package each of red, blue, purple and green Pop Rocks
- 2 cups melted white chocolate
- 3 drops yellow food coloring

xxxxxxxxxxxxxxxxxxxxxxxxxxxxxxxxxxxxxxxxxxxxxxxx

Methods:

1. Set the oven to 350 degrees F.

2. Grease a 9x12 inch baking with cooking oil.

3. Prepare the batter using cake mix as per instructions on the box.

4. Bake for 25 minutes then allows it to cool.

5. Crumble the cake in a bowl. Stir in vanilla icing and mix well.

6. Make small golf ball sized balls out of this mixture.

7. Roll the balls in the pop rocks.

8. Freeze for 30 minutes.

9. Dip the frozen balls in 1 cup white chocolate to coat

10. Mix yellow food color with remaining chocolate and transfer it to a piping bag.

11. Draw small lightning bolts using this mixture on a parchment paper.

12. Allow them to set and dry.

13. Decorate the balls with lightning bolts.

14. Serve.

XXXXXXXXXXXXXXXXXXXXXXXXXXXXXXXXXXXXXXXXXXXXX

Recipe 10 - Pumpkin Pasties

Arranging a Harry Potter themed Halloween party? Then trying these pumpkin pasties is a must. This recipe simple and quick enough to prepare at home. Moreover, you can add variation to the pumpkin filling and change it as per your own taste and style. Serve them as party snack and enjoy the savory flavor.

Serving Size: 16

Prep Time: 10 minutes

Total Prep Time: 25 minutes

List of Ingredients:

For the Dough:

- ½ cup cold ice water
- 2 ½ cups all-purpose flour
- 1 cup salted butter, diced, chilled
- coarse sugar (just for sprinkling)
- 1 beaten egg with 2 tsp. water (egg wash)
- ½ tsp. table salt

For the Filling:

- ¼ cup brown sugar, packed
- 1 cup 100% pure pumpkin puree,
- ¼ tsp. nutmeg
- ¼ tsp. ginger
- 2 TB granulated sugar
- ¼ tsp. cloves
- ½ tsp. cinnamon

For the Glaze/Drizzle:

- 1 TB whole milk
- ½ cup powder sugar
- 1/8 tsp. ginger
- 1/8 tsp. nutmeg
- 1/8 tsp. cinnamon
- 1/8 tsp. cloves

xxxxxxxxxxxxxxxxxxxxxxxxxxxxxxxxxxxxxxxxxxxx

Methods:

1. Mix flour and salt in a bowl. Cut in butter to get cornmeal like mixture.

2. Gradually add ice water while mixing well.

3. Knead the dough well then divide into two equal balls.

4. Wrap each in a plastic sheet and refrigerate for 1 hour.

Make the Filling:

5. Meanwhile, mix all the ingredients for filling in a bowl.

6. Set your oven to 400 degrees F. Layer a baking sheet with parchment paper.

7. Roll the chilled dough balls into 1/8-inch-thick sheets on a floured surface.

8. Cut out 6-inch circles out of these sheets.

9. Use the remaining dough to make more circles.

10. Spoon 2 Tbsp. of the filling at the center of each of circle.

11. Wet the edges and fold the wraps in half. Seal the edges by pressing with a fork.

12. Carve 2 to 3 slits on the wraps and top each with egg wash.

13. Sprinkle sugar and place them on a baking sheet.

14. Bake for 25 minutes until golden brown.

15. Whisk all the glaze ingredients in a glass bowl.

16. Drizzle this glaze on the pasties.

XXXXXXXXXXXXXXXXXXXXXXXXXXXXXXXXXXXXXXXXXXXXXXX

Recipe 11 - Molly's Meatballs and Onion Sauce

Every now and then we love to have some meatballs with our favorite pasta, noodles or rice. The Molly's meatballs recipe is unique in flavor because of its juicy onion sauce. Serve with warm with freshly boiled egg noodles or pasta and enjoy.

Serving Size: 4

Prep Time: 10 minutes

Total Prep Time: 35 minutes

List of Ingredients:

Meatballs:

- ½ cup fresh or dry breadcrumbs
- 1 lb. extra-lean ground beef
- 1 onion, finely chopped
- 1 large egg
- 2 Tbsp. vegetable oil
- 2 Tbsp. chopped fresh parsley
- 1 clove garlic, crushed
- ½ tsp. salt
- 1 tsp. Worcestershire sauce
- 1/8 tsp. nutmeg
- ¼ tsp. freshly ground black pepper

Onion Sauce:

- 2 Tbsp. vegetable oil
- 1 onion, chopped
- 1 Tbsp. all-purpose flour
- 1 (14-oz) can chicken broth
- 1 tsp. Worcestershire sauce
- 1 bay leaf

xxxxxxxxxxxxxxxxxxxxxxxxxxxxxxxxxxxxxxxxxxxxxx

Methods:

1. Combine all the meatballs ingredients in a bowl.

2. Make 1.5-inch small meatballs out of this mixture.

3. Heat oil in a pan. Sear the meatballs for 4 minutes side.

4. Sauté onion in a greased skillet until golden brown.

5. Add flour and stir cook for 1 minute.

6. Pour in broth, Worcestershire sauce, and bay leaf.

7. Stir cook until it thickens.

8. Return the meatballs to the sauce and cook for 15 minutes.

9. Serve with egg noodles.

xxxxxxxxxxxxxxxxxxxxxxxxxxxxxxxxxxxxxxxxxxxxx

Recipe 12 - Treacle Tart

Crumbly and crunchy treacle tarts are just the right thing for every theme party. They are not only delicious to the core, but they have this unique combination of crumbly crust with a creamy filling inside. These mildly sweet tarts are great for after meal desserts.

Serving Size: 12

Prep Time: 10 minutes

Total Prep Time: 35 minutes

List of Ingredients:

For the Crust

- ¼ tsp. salt
- 1 ½ cups all-purpose flour
- 1/3 cup confectioners' sugar
- ½ cup butter, cut into pieces
- 3-4 Tbsp. ice water

For the Filling

- 18 oz. golden syrup
- 2 eggs
- Zest and juice of 1 lemon
- 3/4 tsp. ground ginger
- 2 Tbsp. heavy cream
- 1 cup fresh breadcrumbs

xxxxxxxxxxxxxxxxxxxxxxxxxxxxxxxxxxxxxxxxxxxxx

Methods:

1. Blend flour, salt and sugar in a blender along with cold butter.

2. Gradually add 2 Tbsp. cold water to the flour and blend until well.

3. Stir in more water until it forms a firm dough. Knead well on a floured surface.

4. Make seven-inch disc using this mixture and wrap it in a plastic wrap.

5. Refrigerate for 30 minutes.

6. Divide the dough into small balls and spread them into 1/8-inch-thick tartlets.

7. Layer greased tart pans with the tartlets.

8. Arrange the tart pans on a cookie sheet and refrigerate for 30 minutes.

9. Meanwhile, set the oven to 350 degrees F.

10. Press the tartlet dough and cover them with parchment paper.

11. Add some dry beans for weight and bake for 15 minutes.

12. Combine all the ingredients for filling in a bowl.

13. Divide the filling in the tartlet crusts and bake for 20 minutes.

14. Serve.

xxxxxxxxxxxxxxxxxxxxxxxxxxxxxxxxxxxxxxxxxxxxxx

Recipe 13 - Sorting Hat Cupcakes

Another way to add a vintage sorting hat to the dinner table is the sorting hat cupcake. These are an ordinary cupcake with a magical twist of Harry Potter. So, spread this magic in your kitchen and make these cupcakes with chocolate hats and cookies.

Serving Size: 12

Prep Time: 10 minutes

Total Prep Time: 25 minutes

List of Ingredients:

For Hats

- 12 chocolate kisses
- 6 Oreos, cream removed
- ¼ cup chocolate chips, melted

For buttercream

- ¼ cup heavy cream
- 1 ½ cups butter, softened
- 6 cups powdered sugar
- 2 Tbsp. Butterscotch syrup
- Pinch kosher salt
- Red, yellow, green, and blue food coloring
- Gold sprinkles, for garnish
- 1 box white cake mix,

xxxxxxxxxxxxxxxxxxxxxxxxxxxxxxxxxxxxxxxxxxxxxxx

Methods:

1. Set the oven to 350 degrees F.

2. Line a muffin tray with paper liners.

3. Prepare batter using the cake mix as per the instructions on the box.

4. Divide the batter into the liner and bake for 25 minutes.

5. Allow the cupcakes to cool.

6. Meanwhile, make small hats using chocolate shred at the center of Oreo cookie.

7. Allow them to sit for 15 minutes.

8. Blend butter with sugar, cream, butterscotch, and salt until creamy.

9. Reserve 1/3 of the frosting and divide the remaining frosting into 4 separate bowls.

10. Add red, blue, green and yellow food color to each of the four bowls.

11. Mix well and fill the center of the cupcakes with the colorful frosting.

12. Top each cupcake with white buttercream and gold sprinkles.

13. Place chocolate hats on top and serve.

xxxxxxxxxxxxxxxxxxxxxxxxxxxxxxxxxxxxxxxxxxxxxxx

Recipe 14 - Peppermint Toads

No Harry Potter theme menu is complete without some toads at the dinner or snack table. These peppermint toads are not only special in taste but also looks inviting. A great combination of white chocolate with marshmallow crème is what these little toads are all about.

Serving Size: 6

Prep Time: 10 minutes

Total Prep Time: 5 minutes

List of Ingredients:

- 1 ½ cups white chocolate
- ½ cup marshmallow creme
- 1 Tbsp. Honey
- 2 Tbsp. Shortening
- Peppermint flavor
- Red food coloring
- A frog/toad-shaped candy mold
- Microwave-safe bowls
- Spoons
- A Ziplock bag

xxxxxxxxxxxxxxxxxxxxxxxxxxxxxxxxxxxxxxxxxxxxxxx

Methods:

1. Melt ½ cup white chocolate in a bowl by heating in a microwave for 1 minute.

2. Add the melted chocolate to a Ziplock bag and smoosh it to one corner of the bag.

3. Cut the corner's tip and pipe the white chocolate into diagonal lines in a frog mold.

4. Refrigerate the molds for 20 to 30 minutes until it hardens.

5. Meanwhile, melt the remaining white chocolate in a bowl.

6. Stir in marshmallow crème, food coloring, peppermint flavor, and honey. Mix well.

7. Divide the peppermint mixture into the refrigerated frog molds.

8. Refrigerate again for 30 minutes.

9. Serve.

XXXXXXXXXXXXXXXXXXXXXXXXXXXXXXXXXXXXXXXXXXXX

Recipe 15 - Lemon, Cheesecake with Vanilla Wafer

Want to try something trendy for the party? Try this lemon cheesecake with crumbly wafer crust. The recipe is quick and easy. Blend, assemble and bake, three steps, and you are done. Decorate with your favorite icing on top.

Serving Size: 16

Prep Time: 10 minutes

Total Prep Time: 50 minutes

List of Ingredients:

Ingredients for the crust:

- 1 ½ cups vanilla wafer crumbs
- ¼ cup plus 1 Tbsp. unsalted butter, melted
- 2 Tbsp. granulated sugar

Ingredients for the filling:

- 2 (8-ounce) packages cream cheese
- 1 cup granulated sugar
- 1 cup sour cream
- 3 egg, room temperature
- 1 tsp. vanilla extract
- 1 tsp. lemon extract
- 2 Tbsp. lemon juice
- Zest of 1 lemon

XXXXXXXXXXXXXXXXXXXXXXXXXXXXXXXXXXXXXXXXXXXXX

Methods:

1. Heat your oven to 325 degrees F. Butter an 8-inch springform pan.

2. Cover the springform with foil sheet from outside.

3. Combine cookie crumbs with sugar, and butter in a bowl.

4. Pour this mixture into the pan and press it firmly against the bottom.

5. Preparing the Filling:

6. Blend cream with sugar and cream cheese until smooth.

7. Stir in vanilla, sour cream, lemon extract, lemon zest, and juice.

8. Mix well at medium-high speed.

9. Gradually whisk in eggs while blending the mixture.

10. Pour this filling into the crust.

11. Bake for 50 minutes.

12. Allow it to cool for 1 hour.

13. Slice and serve.

XXXXXXXXXXXXXXXXXXXXXXXXXXXXXXXXXXXXXXXXXXXXXXXX

Recipe 16 - Treacle Tart with Rosemary and Lemon

Add a little twist to the old treacle tart recipe with the added freshness and aroma of lemon and rosemary. This tart, in particular, is famous for its juicy, delicious filling loaded with corn syrup, breadcrumbs and almond meal.

Serving Size: 12

Prep Time: 10 minutes

Total Prep Time: 50 minutes

List of Ingredients:

For the tart base:

- 1 cup plain flour
- ¾ stick butter
- pinch of salt
- 2-3 Tbsp. cold water

For the filling:

- ¼ stick butter
- zest and juice of half a lemon
- ⅔ cup + 1Tbsp. Lyle's Golden Corn Syrup
- 1 tsp. finely chopped rosemary
- 1 + ¼ cups fresh breadcrumbs
- ⅔ cup almond meal
- 1 egg

xxxxxxxxxxxxxxxxxxxxxxxxxxxxxxxxxxxxxxxxxxxxxxx

Methods:

1. Set your oven to 375 degrees F. Grease a 9.5-inch cake pan.

2. Blend flour with butter in a blender until crumbly.

3. Gradually add water to the flour and mix to form a soft dough.

4. Press the dough in the baking dish and bake for 30 minutes until golden brown.

5. Meanwhile, melt butter in a medium saucepan until it turns brown.

6. Stir in all the remaining ingredients for filling except egg.

7. Whisk well and cook on low heat until well mixed.

8. Whisk in egg and divide the mixture into the baked base.

9. Bake for another 20 minutes.

10. Allow it cool for 15 minutes then slice and serve.

xxxxxxxxxxxxxxxxxxxxxxxxxxxxxxxxxxxxxxxxxxxxxxx

Recipe 17 - Lemon Drop Candies

Candies are loved by all for their sweet and savory flavor. These yellow lemon drops are made out of sugar and lemon and citric extracts which gives them a nice blend of sweet with sour. Make as many in a single batch and store in a sealed container for later use.

Serving Size: 20

Prep Time: 10 minutes

Total Prep Time: 10 minutes

List of Ingredients:

- ½ cup water
- powdered or granulated sugar, to coat
- 1 cup sugar, granulated
- ½ tsp. lemon extract
- ½ tsp. cream of tartar
- yellow gel food coloring
- 2 tsp. citric acid

xxxxxxxxxxxxxxxxxxxxxxxxxxxxxxxxxxxxxxxxxxxx

Methods:

1. Mix sugar with water and cream of tartar in a saucepan over medium heat.

2. Cook until the temperature turns to 300 degrees F.

3. Pour this mixture into a silicon mold.

4. Stir in citric acid, lemon extract, and gel coloring.

5. Mix well and allow it to cool for 5 minutes.

6. Make long ropes using this mixture.

7. Cut the ropes into small sticks and roll them in sugar.

8. Serve.

xxxxxxxxxxxxxxxxxxxxxxxxxxxxxxxxxxxxxxxxxxxxx

Recipe 18 - Butterbeer and Ice Cream Floats

Treat yourself with the ultimate mug of happiness. It has practically everything we all die for, cream, ice cream, and butterbeer. It serves as an excellent beverage for the table when there are special celebrations around. It's warming and soothing to the core. It does take a little extra time and ingredients, but it will be all worth it.

Serving Size: 4

Prep Time: 10 minutes

Total Prep Time: 20 minutes

List of Ingredients:

Dark Butterscotch Caramel Sauce:

- 1 cup whole milk
- 1 3/4 cups dark brown sugar
- ¼ cup butter
- ½ cup heavy whipping cream
- 1 tsp. sea salt
- 2 Tbsp. molasses
- 2 tsp. vanilla extract
- 2 Tbsp. Scotch whiskey

No-Churn Caramel Coconut Ice Cream:

- 4 cups whole milk
- 1 ½ cups sugar
- 2 cups full-fat coconut milk
- ¼ cup cornstarch
- 8 egg yolks
- 4 Tbsp. butter
- ½ tsp. salt
- 2 tsp. vanilla
- ¼ cup prepared caramel

Butterbeer

- 1 ½ cups carbonated water
- ¼ tsp. vanilla extract
- 3 ½ Tbsp. prepared caramel
- 1 Tbsp. whipping cream
- 1 tsp. strong black coffee
- ½ tsp. cocoa powder
- 3 - 4 drops cider vinegar
- 1 dash salt
- 1 dash nutmeg
- 1 dash cinnamon
- 1 dash ginger

xxxxxxxxxxxxxxxxxxxxxxxxxxxxxxxxxxxxxxxxxxxxx

Methods:

Caramel:

1. Mix brown sugar with milk, butter, cream, salt and molasses in a saucepan on medium heat.

2. Boil the mixture and stir cook for 10 minutes until it darkens.

3. Stir in bourbon then reduce the heat. Cook for 5 minutes.

4. Add vanilla and mix well. Allow it cool and store in a sealed container.

No-Churn Coconut Caramel Ice Cream:

5. Beat egg yolks with sugar in a large bowl.

6. Stir in salt, cornstarch, and milk.

7. Transfer the mixture to a cooking pan.

8. Stir cook for 8 minutes on low heat then turns off the heat.

9. Add vanilla, caramel, and butter and mix well.

10. Strain the mixture through the mesh strainer into a container.

11. Refrigerate for 30 minutes. Meanwhile, beat coconut milk until fluffy.

12. Pour the cream into ice cream mixture and mix well. Freeze overnight.

Butterbeer Floats:

13. Mix all the ingredients for butterbeer except carbonated water at the bottom of a mug.

14. Add a cup of carbonated water and place 2 scoops of coconut ice cream.

15. Serve immediately.

XXXXXXXXXXXXXXXXXXXXXXXXXXXXXXXXXXXXXXXXXXXXXX

Recipe 19 - Hogwarts House Cup Chicken

Enjoy the juicily roasted chicken drumstick at home using this tasty Hogwarts house cup chicken recipe. It has basic seasoning including garlic, onion powder, salt, and pepper. Honey and lemon juice add a sweet juicy feel to every bite.

Serving Size: 12

Prep Time: 10 minutes

Total Prep Time: 20 minutes

List of Ingredients:

- 12 chicken drumsticks
- 2 tsp. dried basil
- Garlic powder, to taste
- Onion powder, to taste
- Salt, to taste
- Black pepper, to taste
- 4 Tbsp.
- 2 Tbsp. honey

xxxxxxxxxxxxxxxxxxxxxxxxxxxxxxxxxxxxxxxxxxxxxx

Methods:

1. Rub the drumsticks with salt, olive oil, pepper, onion powder, and garlic powder.

2. Arrange the drumsticks on a baking sheet in a single layer.

3. Sprinkle dried basil on top.

4. Mix honey with lemon juice and pour over the chicken.

5. Bake for 20 minutes at 375 degrees.

6. Rotate the drumsticks and bake for 20 minutes.

7. Serve warm.

xxxxxxxxxxxxxxxxxxxxxxxxxxxxxxxxxxxxxxxxxxxxxx

Recipe 20 - Pomphrey's Pumpkin Juice Smoothie

Who doesn't like a fresh dose of smoothie on a beautiful evening? This pumpkin juice is extra special due to its richness, color, and flavor. It has the added nutrients of apples, carrot, and orange alongside the pumpkin. It is simply great for the kids, and they would enjoy it on their Harry Potter theme celebrations.

Serving Size: 4

Prep Time: 10 minutes

Total Prep Time: 20 minutes

List of Ingredients:

- 1 cup cooked pumpkin puree
- ½ tsp. cloves, ground
- 2 carrot, chopped
- 1 tsp. vanilla extract
- 2/3 cup coconut milk
- 2 apples, peeled and cored
- 2 cup water
- 2 orange, peeled and cut into sections
- 2 bananas, peeled
- 1 tsp. cider vinegar
- 2 tsp. cinnamon

XXXXXXXXXXXXXXXXXXXXXXXXXXXXXXXXXXXXXXXXXXXXX

Methods:

1. Blend all the ingredients in a blender.

2. Refrigerate for 1 to 2 hours.

3. Serve.

XXXXXXXXXXXXXXXXXXXXXXXXXXXXXXXXXXXXXXXXXXXXX

Recipe 21 - Treacle Toffee Recipe

Make these black molasses toffees to serve on the table. These are made out of simple sugar mixture which mixed and cooled. Toffees can be stored in bite-size pieces in a sealed jar for days. Preserve in the refrigerator and serve whenever needed.

Serving Size: 6

Prep Time: 10 minutes

Total Prep Time: 10 minutes

List of Ingredients:

- 1lb dark brown sugar
- ¼ pint water
- ¼ tsp. cream of tartar
- ½ cup black molasses
- ½ cup corn syrup

XXXXXXXXXXXXXXXXXXXXXXXXXXXXXXXXXXXXXXXXXXXXX

Methods:

1. Grease 30x10 cm pan with butter.

2. Mix sugar in water in a cooking pot over low heat.

3. Stir in all the remaining ingredients and bring it to a boil.

4. Pour this mixture into the greased pan.

5. Allow it to cool until firm.

6. Break the toffee into bite-size pieces.

7. Serve.

XXXXXXXXXXXXXXXXXXXXXXXXXXXXXXXXXXXXXXXXXXXXX

Recipe 22 - Double Chocolate Cauldron Cakes

Cauldron cake is particularly popular in the Harry Potter menu for their adorable outlook and amazing flavor. Mothers all around the world are going extra miles to get its perfect recipe to surprise their little harry fans on special celebrations. They contain the goodness of chocolate and the cakes and serve as a nourishing dessert for every table.

Serving Size: 6

Prep Time: 10 minutes

Total Prep Time: 20 minutes

List of Ingredients:

For the Cakes

- 2 cups all-purpose flour
- 3/4 cup cocoa powder
- 1 ½ tsp. baking powder
- ½ tsp. baking soda
- 1 tsp. salt
- ½ cup canola oil
- 2 cups sugar
- 1 egg
- 1 tsp. vanilla
- 1 cup milk
- 1 cup semi-sweet chocolate chips

For the Filling

- ½ cup butter
- ½ cup sugar
- ½ cup milk
- 4 ½ tsp. all-purpose flour
- 4 ½ tsp. powdered chocolate milk mix
- ½ tsp. vanilla

For the Frosting

- 1 cup butter
- 4 cups confectioners' sugar
- 1 ¼ cups cocoa powder
- ½ tsp. vanilla
- ¼ to ½ cup milk

XXXXXXXXXXXXXXXXXXXXXXXXXXXXXXXXXXXXXXXXXXXX

Methods:

Cake:

1. Set your oven to 350 degrees F. Layer a muffin tray with paper liners.

2. Mix flour with baking powder, cocoa, salt and baking powder in a bowl.

3. Beat oil with sugar in a mixing bowl. Whisk in egg and vanilla.

4. Gradually add flour mixture and milk alternatively while blending.

5. Fold in chocolate chips and add 2 Tbsp. of the batter into each muffin cup.

6. Bake for about 20 minutes.

To make the filling:

7. Mix milk with chocolate drink mix and flour in a saucepan over medium-high heat.

8. Stir cook until it thickens then turn off the heat. Allow it to cool.

9. Blend sugar and butter in an electric mixer until fluffy.

10. Stir in vanilla and milk mixture.

To make the frosting:

11. Blend butter with sugar in a mixer and stir in cocoa and vanilla.

12. Gradually add milk while beating until fluffy.

Assembling:

13. Dip the base of each muffin cake into melted chocolate.

14. Carve a groove at the center of each muffin base.

15. Divide the filling into each groove and top each with frosting.

16. Make cauldron handles by piping melted chocolate over parchment paper into U shape.

17. Allow them to cool and dry.

18. Fix these handles in the cauldrons and serve.

xxxxxxxxxxxxxxxxxxxxxxxxxxxxxxxxxxxxxxxxxxxx

Recipe 23 - Special Pudding

This pudding is best to serve on Halloween parties, and special Potter inspired theme parties. It is cooked well on simmering water. Unlike ordinary pudding, it is rich in dried fruits, apple, almonds, and crumbs which gives it a crunchy texture.

Serving Size: 12

Prep Time: 10 minutes

Total Prep Time: 7 hours

List of Ingredients:

- 1-ounce candied peel (mixed varieties, finely chopped)
- 1-pound mixed dried fruit
- 1 Tbsp. orange zest
- 1 small apple (cooking apple, peeled, cored and chopped finely)
- 2 Tbsp. orange juice
- ½ Tbsp. lemon zest
- 4 Tbsp. brandy
- 1 Tbsp. lemon juice
- 1 tsp. mixed spice (level, ground)
- 2 ounces flour (self-raising, sifted)
- 4 ounces suet vegetarian, shredded
- 1 ½ tsp. cinnamon (ground)
- 4 ounces breadcrumbs (white, fresh)
- 4 ounces brown sugar (dark, soft)
- 2 large eggs (fresh)
- 1-ounce almonds (whole, shelled, roughly chopped)

XXXXXXXXXXXXXXXXXXXXXXXXXXXXXXXXXXXXXXXXXXXXX

Methods:

1. Grease a 2.5-pint pudding basin with butter.

2. Mix candied peel with apple, dried fruits, lemon juice and orange juice in a mixing bowl.

3. Stir in brandy and cover the bowl. Marinate overnight.

4. Mix flour with cinnamon and mixed spice in a bowl.

5. Stir in sugar, lemon, orange zest, nuts, suet, and breadcrumbs. Mix well.

6. Add marinated dried fruits and mix well.

7. Beat eggs in a bowl and stir in all the dry ingredients.

8. Transfer the mixture to the pudding basin and cook over simmering water for 7 hours.

9. Stir well after every 15 minutes.

10. Allow it to cool then serve.

XXXXXXXXXXXXXXXXXXXXXXXXXXXXXXXXXXXXXXXXXXXXX

Recipe 24 - Cheese and Pretzel Broomsticks

We can't even imagine a wizard without a broomstick. That is why this simple recipe brings cheese broomsticks to your special menu. Making use of sheer creativity, you can turn your cheese slices and stored pretzels into something so fascinating and delicious. Serve them either a snack or an appetizer.

Serving Size: 12

Prep Time: 10 minutes

Total Prep Time: 0 minutes

List of Ingredients:

- 12 stick pretzels
- 6 cheese slices
- 3 shallots, green parts only

xxxxxxxxxxxxxxxxxxxxxxxxxxxxxxxxxxxxxxxxxxxxxx

Methods:

1. Cut the cheese slices in half and make fringes at one end of each slice.

2. Wrap the fringed slices one end of the pretzel with fringes on the other end.

3. Slice thin strips out of the green part of the shallot.

4. Secure the cheese wraps using these thin strips.

5. Serve.

xxxxxxxxxxxxxxxxxxxxxxxxxxxxxxxxxxxxxxxxxxxxxx

Recipe 25 - Chocolate Frogs

These are simple chocolate frogs which you can prepare in just a few minutes. With simple steps and basic ingredients, you can enjoy peanut butter filled chocolate toads at home. Chill well before serving to enjoy the best of its flavor.

Serving Size: 8

Prep Time: 10 minutes

Total Prep Time: 02 minutes

List of Ingredients:

- 1-pound milk chocolate

Peanut Butter Filling:

- ½ cup natural peanut butter
- ¼ cup + 2 Tbsp. confectioners' sugar
- 1/8 tsp. salt
- Special equipment: frog shaped mold

Methods:

1. Melt chocolate in a bowl by heating in the microwave for 30 seconds.

2. Pour this melt into the frog molds. Allow it to cool.

3. Combine all the filling ingredients in a glass bowl.

4. Stuff the chocolate molds with the filling and press it gently into the molds.

5. Refrigerate for 30 minutes.

6. Serve.

xxxxxxxxxxxxxxxxxxxxxxxxxxxxxxxxxxxxxxxxxxxxxxx

Recipe 26 - Golden Snitch Cake Pops

The golden snitch ball is what everyone is running after, at least in all the Harry Potter series. Today every Harry one is as much crazy about the snitch. These snitch cake pops are for all such lovers. These are made of simple cake recipes and then later coated with layers of pops, frosting, and customized lightning bolts.

Serving Size: 6

Prep Time: 10 minutes

Total Prep Time: 20 minutes

List of Ingredients:

- 1 tub store-bought frosting
- 1 box cake mix (+ required eggs and oil)
- Lollipop sticks
- Yellow candy melts
- White fondant
- Gold sprinkles (we bought this at Williams & Sonoma)

xxxxxxxxxxxxxxxxxxxxxxxxxxxxxxxxxxxxxxxxxx

Methods:

1. Make cake pops as per the given instructions on the box.

2. Roll the cake pops in the yellow candy melts. Allow it cool.

3. Coat the balls with gold sprinkles.

4. Using a sharp knife cut the wings out of white fondant.

5. Fix the wings in the cake pops and serve.

xxxxxxxxxxxxxxxxxxxxxxxxxxxxxxxxxxxxxxxxxx

Recipe 27 - Monster Book Snacks

There are never-ending ways to make your cuisine look like Harry inspired and these monster book cookies are another way to nicely add an important part of the series to the table. These cookies are rich in chocolate, marshmallows, icings and graham crackers. Serve them with warm milk and the kids will love it.

Serving Size: 12

Prep Time: 10 minutes

Total Prep Time: 20 minutes

List of Ingredients:

- 24 graham cracker cookies
- 1 cup mini Marshmallow
- 1 cup melted chocolate
- ½ cup chocolate shreds
- ¼ cup M&Ms

xxxxxxxxxxxxxxxxxxxxxxxxxxxxxxxxxxxxxxxxxxxxxxxx

Methods:

1. Dip graham cracker in melted chocolate. Allow them to cool.

2. Spread icing on one side of the graham cracker.

3. Place marshmallows on the icing side of half of the graham cracker to make the teeth.

4. Place the remaining half of the graham crackers over the marshmallows with their icing side down.

5. Top the crackers with chocolate shreds.

6. Make book eyes with M&Ms and serve.

xxxxxxxxxxxxxxxxxxxxxxxxxxxxxxxxxxxxxxxxxxxx

Recipe 28 - Polyjuice Potion Jelly Shots

Jelly shots are a fun way to incorporate Harry inspired recipe into your menu. These are colorful giggly delights which are made out of the delicious combinations of the ginger ale, pineapple juice, and lemon. They are great to serve as party snacks or a side dish on the dinner table.

Serving Size: 12

Prep Time: 10 minutes

Total Prep Time: 15 minutes

List of Ingredients:

- Ginger Ale mixture
- ½ cup ginger ale
- 1 envelope plain gelatin
- ½ cup ginger vodka
- Pineapple mixture
- ½ cup canned pineapple juice
- 1 envelope plain gelatin
- ½ cup pineapple vodka
- Lime mixture
- ½ cup water
- 1 envelope plain gelatin
- ½ cup lime sherbet, melted

xxxxxxxxxxxxxxxxxxxxxxxxxxxxxxxxxxxxxxxxxxx

Methods:

1. Soak gelatin in ginger ale in a saucepan for 2 minutes.

2. Stir cook for 5 minutes on low heat then turns off the heat.

3. Add vodka and mix well.

4. Soak gelatin in pineapple juice in a saucepan for 2 minutes.

5. Stir cook for 5 minutes on low heat then turn off the heat.

6. Add vodka and mix well.

7. Soak gelatin in water in a saucepan for 2 minutes.

8. Stir cook for 5 minutes on low heat then turn off the heat.

9. Add melted sherbet and mix well.

10. Divide the three mixtures into silicone molds.

11. Allow them to cool and serve.

XXXXXXXXXXXXXXXXXXXXXXXXXXXXXXXXXXXXXXXXXXXXX

Recipe 29 - Harry Potter Pumpkin Howler

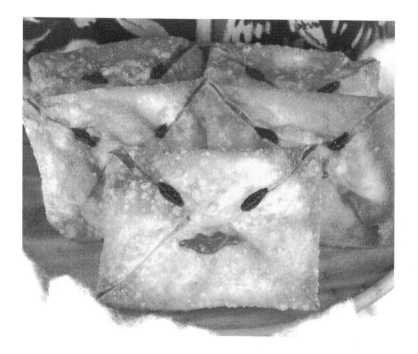

Another snack to try for the table. These are simple egg roll wrappers filled with creamy mascarpone filling but shaped in a nice Harry inspiring howler with icing eyes and lips drawn on the outside. Serve fresh and enjoy your favorite smoothies or drink in the evening.

Serving Size: 12

Prep Time: 10 minutes

Total Prep Time: 10 minutes

List of Ingredients:

Filling:

- ¼ tsp. cinnamon
- 1 Tbsp. brown sugar
- 2 Tbsp. pumpkin puree
- 8 oz. mascarpone cheese
- Pinch of salt
- Dash of nutmeg

Howlers Wrap

- 3 egg roll wrappers, sliced in quarter pieces
- Red icing
- Black icing
- Oil for frying
- 1 beaten egg with 1 tsp. water (egg wash)
- 12 eggroll wrappers

xxxxxxxxxxxxxxxxxxxxxxxxxxxxxxxxxxxxxxxxxxxxxx

Methods:

1. Mix pumpkin with mascarpone cheese, cinnamon, salt, nutmeg, and brown sugar.

2. Spread the egg roll wrappers with their pointed side upward.

3. Add a Tbsp. of cheese is filling at the center of each.

4. Wet the edges with egg wash and wrap to form small envelopes.

5. Heat oil in a deep pan on medium heat.

6. Cook them in hot oil until golden brown.

7. Make eyes using black icing on each envelope and make lip using red icing.

8. Serve.

XXXXXXXXXXXXXXXXXXXXXXXXXXXXXXXXXXXXXXXXXXXX

Recipe 30 - Gillyweed Stalks

Health is always the first priority we all share as a parent. And there is no better delicious way to add zucchini to the home cuisine. Here the zucchini slices are seasoned and then grilled which gives it a strong aroma and earthly taste. Try these with your favorite dip or sauce.

Serving Size: 2

Prep Time: 10 minutes

Total Prep Time: 20 minutes

List of Ingredients:

- 2 zucchinis, sliced longitudinally
- 2 Tbsp. olive oil
- Garlic salt, to taste.

Methods:

1. Season the zucchini slices with garlic salt and 2 Tbsp. olive oil.

2. Refrigerate for 2 hrs. for marination.

3. Meanwhile, preheat a grill on medium heat.

4. Grill the zucchini slices for 2 minutes per side.

5. Serve.

xxxxxxxxxxxxxxxxxxxxxxxxxxxxxxxxxxxxxxxxxxxx

Made in the USA
Coppell, TX
24 November 2019

11736843R00062